MORE FUN THAN BOWLING

BY

Steven Dietz

S A M U E L F R E N C H , I N C .

45 WEST 25TH STREET   NEW YORK 10010
7623 SUNSET BOULEVARD   HOLLYWOOD 90046
LONDON   *TORONTO*

FOR MY PARENTS –
IRENE LIND DIETZ
AND
JOHN VICTOR DIETZ

IMPORTANT BILLING AND CREDIT REQUIREMENTS

All producers of MORE FUN THAN BOWLING *must* give credit to the Author of the Play in all programs distributed in connection with performances of the Play and in all instances in which the title of the Play appears for purposes of advertising, publicizing or otherwise exploiting the Play and/or a production. The name of the Author *must* also appear on a separate line, on which no other name appears, immediately following the title, and *must* appear in size of type not less than fifty percent the size of the title type.

Please note:

Mention is made of songs which are *not* in the
public domain. Producers of this play are hereby
CAUTIONED that permission to produce this play
does not include rights to use these songs in
production. Producers should contact the
copyright owners directly for rights.

More Fun Than Bowling received its premiere production at Actors Theatre of St. Paul, St. Paul, Minnesota. Michael Andrew Miner, artistic director.

This production was directed by George C. White. The set was designed by Dick Leerhoff, lights by Nayna Ramey, and costumes by Chris Johnson. The stage manager was Jeff Couture.

The cast was as follows:

JAKE TOMLINSON	James Cada
MOLLY TOMLINSON	Annie Enneking
LOIS	Terry Heck
LORETTA	Nanci Olesen
MISTER DYSON	John Seibert

The author wishes to thank the Playwrights' Center, Minneapolis, and the Manitoba Association of Playwrights, Winnepeg, for their developmental support.

CHARACTERS

JAKE TOMLINSON ....40, owner of the Dust
    Bowl
MOLLY..........................16, Jake's daughter
LOIS..............30, Jake's second wife, Molly's
    stepmother
LORETTA ...28, Jake's third wife, also Molly's
    stepmother
MISTER DYSON.................. 28, a chauffeur

TIME

May of the present, and moments from the past

PLACE

A hill overlooking the small midwestern town of
Turtle Rapids

and I wish you'd a known her
we were quite a pair
she was sharp as a razor
and soft as a prayer

Tom Waits
"Bad Liver and a Broken Heart"

ACT I

SCENE: Three large mounds of dirt facing the audience. Graves without headstones. Grass surrounding them.

A path goes down the hill Stage Right.

Upstage, among an assortment of large trees is an area known as The Shadows. It is always in darkness.

Far Upstage is a cyclorama which will depict the passage of time from sunrise to moonrise.

AT RISE: Mist covers the graves. A rooster CROWS. Birds begin to CHIRP. The SUN rises and with it the LIGHTS come up on MISTER DYSON standing directly in front of the center grave.

MISTER DYSON wears a black suit, black shirt, black hat, black shoes, black gloves, dark sunglasses and a bright blood-red tie.

HE has a black briefcase handcuffed to one wrist. In the other hand he holds a revolver.

HE loads the revolver gracefully during the following.

DYSON. (*Directly to audience.*) My name is Mister Dyson. Please call me that. I am here to find a Mister Jake Tomlinson. It is important that I speak to him. I must find the proper moment. Timing is crucial. As with driving a vehicle in heavy traffic, the moment of acceleration or de-acceleration almost exclusively determines the success or failure of a multi-lane maneuver. (*Pause.*) You can't just close your eyes and gun it.

(*A SOUND from offstage. Perhaps a bicycle BELL, two rings.*)

DYSON. That is all I can say to you right now. (*Retreats quickly and hides in The Shadows.*)

(*MOLLY enters up the path on her bike. SHE stops, dismounts, and locks the wheels with a chain and padlock.*)

MOLLY. (*Singing.*)
Pack up all my care and woe
here I go, singin' low
Bye Bye Blackbird

Where somebody waits for me
sugar's sweet, so is he
Bye Bye Blackbird

(*In a basket on the bike are two bowling pins with brightly colored pinwheels rising out of the*

*tops of them. MOLLY puts one of these bowling
pinwheels at the Upstage head of the Stage
Right grave, stands behind it, and speaks to
the grave.)*

MOLLY. Happy birthday, Mom. I miss you.
(*Sings again.*)
No one here can love or understand me
Oh what hard luck stories they all hand me ...

(*SHE advances to the middle grave, looks at it,
stops singing. SHE starts to put the second
pinwheel down.   Stops. Reconsiders. SHE
walks off the distance from the first grave to
the middle grave and does not seem satisfied
with her findings. SHE walks off the distance
from the first grave to the Stage Left grave and
seems convinced. SHE sings again as she
puts the second pinwheel at the Upstage head of
the Stage Left grave.*)

MOLLY. (*Singing.*)
Make my bed and light the light
I'll be home late tonight
Blackbird Bye Bye
(*Stops, speaks to Stage Left grave.*) Happy
birthday, Mom. I miss you.

(*SHE steps back, looks at the two pinwheels.
Kneels down and looks at the middle grave,
runs her finger through the dirt, pulls out a*

*small plastic straw and discards it casually,
crumbles a dirt clod in her hand, and then
stands and moves to her bike. SHE unlocks
the bike and rides away down the hill.*
Short pause.
*With numerous grunts and groans and inaudible
expletives, JAKE emerges from the middle
grave. HE is obviously covered with dirt from
head to toe.)*

JAKE. (*Furious.*) J.C. CHRIST! THEY'RE
TRYIN' TO KILL ME. I'M TRYIN' LIKE HELL
TO SEE WHAT IT'S LIKE TO BE DEAD AND
SOMEONE'S TRYIN' TO KILL ME! Don't turn
your back on a person with a fetish for straws, let
me tell you twice. They're the kind that walk by,
look at a mound of dirt, see a straw, and yank it
out of your mouth. They're the kind that take
fifteen out of the dispenser at McDonald's because
they're *free*. Keep 'em in their glove compartment
and never use 'em. I hate people like that. You
know what else I hate? People that ask for five
ketchups, use three and put two in their glove
compartment. Quote me – that kind of deception
will catch up with you. ASK FOR WHAT YOU
NEED – NOT A LITTLE EXTRA TO STORE
AWAY FOR A RAINY DAY. Those were my
momma's words to live by and she should know
because she spent her last five dollars two hours
before she died – leavin' me with nothin'. She
made both columns come up even. She understood

that straws and ketchup don't mean shit on a rainy day. (*Pause, calms a bit, brushes dirt off, tips his feed cap to audience.*) Jake Tomlinson. You sorta caught the tail end of my experiment. See, WHOEVER KNOWS THINGS is fixin' to end my life and when that happens I'm gonna have to live there in that grave for a longer time than I care to think about. So, I thought I'd try to get the flavor of it so maybe I'd have a better outlook on gettin' killed. Didn't work. Pretty damn boring down there. And I even had a magazine. (*Looks at the two remaining graves.*) I got no idea how Lois and Loretta can stand it. (*Points.*) That's them there. (*Points again.*) Lois and Lor – (*Points again.*) Loretta and Lo – (*Pause.*) That's them there. I used to know which was which, but then they started movin' around to piss me off. LIFE'S A GODDAMN SHELL GAME – PAY ATTENTION OR YOU'LL BE LEFT HOLDIN' AN EMPTY. Those were my father's words to live by and he should know because he held a lot of empties in his day before passing out on some of the finest floors in this country. My momma took her last five dollars and bought him a dog to keep him company, and he named it "Five" so he'd remember its value. And when he got inspired after hearing Pastor Sodderburger preach at my momma's funeral he walked on water halfway across Moby Lake with Five paddlin' right beside him. He was truly in all his glory until he stopped, looked down, and said "I'M WALKIN'

ON THE GODDAMN WATER!" ... at which
point he sank immediately. He rose several
times, gasping for breath and yelling at Five to
"FETCH HELP! FETCH HELP!" ... and then
drowned with Five paddling in a circle around
him with little sticks in her mouth. She obviously
misunderstood. (*HE walks up to one of the
pinwheels and flicks it. It spins. To one of the
graves.*)You always loved flowers, didn't you,
Loretta? (*To the other grave.*) Yeah, you did. I
remember. Except roses. You always hated roses.
Or Lois did. (*Other grave.*) Did you hate roses,
Lois? Yeah, you'd shred 'em and make tea. (*Other
grave.*) Yeah. You did. (*Other grave.*) Well, *one*
of you did. I *do* know that whichever one of you
hated roses was the same one that threw the
electric skillet at me when I wanted to name the
alley the Rose Bowl. (*To audience.*) So, I named it
the Dust Bowl instead.

(*JAKE digs in the dirt that he rose from and pulls
out a shovel, a rake, a lawn chair and a
Reader's Digest. HE tosses the tools to the side,
sets up the lawn chair on the dirt between the
two remaining graves, and sits down with a
sigh. HE takes a pair of small reading
glasses out of his pocket, puts them on, and
cracks open the* Reader's Digest.
DYSON appears from The Shadows.)

JAKE. I've decided I've got no choice but to sit here and square off with whoever's lookin' to kill me. I ain't gonna go without a fight. (*Leans back.*) AAAAAHHHHHHHHHH. This is nice. Sun coming up. Birds chirpin'. Leaves rustlin'. Brand new *Reader's Digest* that's never been in a bathroom. The whole town of Turtle Rapids laid out below me. God, if I had a Fresca right now I could die happy.

(*MOLLY enters quickly on her bike, riding very near DYSON and sending him back into The Shadows. MOLLY has another bowling pinwheel in the basket of her bike. SHE locks the bike and walks up behind Jake – who is not aware of her. SHE puts her arm quickly around his head from behind and says:*)

MOLLY. Hi, Dad.

JAKE. (*Standing and hurling the* Reader's Digest *at Molly*) DIE, SUCKER! (*Pause, JAKE sees it is her.*) Oh, shit. Molly. It's you. Sorry. I didn't know it was you.

MOLLY. Dad, you gotta beat this paranoia thing.

JAKE. You'd be paranoid too if everyone was trying to kill *you*. (*Pause.*) What's that?

MOLLY. (*Putting it ceremonially in his lap, mock serious.*) Bowling pinwheel.

JAKE. I can see that. Didn't know we had any left.

MOLLY. Made a hundred for the County Fair.

JAKE. Thought we sold 'em all.

MOLLY. All but three.

JAKE. Why'd you bring it up here?

MOLLY. To decorate your grave.

JAKE. Yeah?

MOLLY. Yeah.

JAKE. You think that's funny, don't you?

MOLLY. (*Giggles a bit.*) Sort of, yeah.

JAKE. Why?

MOLLY. I came up to visit Lois and Loretta and there was a grave between them – so I figured you'd forgotten their birthday, felt bad and died.

JAKE. You're kidding me, right?

MOLLY. Yeah. I knew it wasn't you. Thought maybe you'd got married again.

JAKE. Molly.

MOLLY. Sorry. Whose grave is it?

JAKE. Mine. I was takin' a trial run. And I was doin' just fine till someone yanked the straw out of my mouth. (*Pause.*)

MOLLY. You were under there?

JAKE. Yeah.

MOLLY. Well, how was I supposed to know?

JAKE. Did you take the straw out of my mouth?

MOLLY. You wanted a trial run.

JAKE. MOLLY — (*Calms himself.*) Did you grieve?

MOLLY. When?

JAKE. When you thought I was dead.

MOLLY. I rode down and got another pinwheel.

JAKE. You really think this is funny, don't you?

MOLLY. Lighten up, Dad. It's okay.

JAKE. You don't know about the prophecy, Molly.

MOLLY. Prophecy?

JAKE. (*Secretly, leading her Downstage away from the graves.*) No one knows this.

MOLLY. I won't tell anyone.

(*DYSON appears from The Shadows, eavesdropping.*)

JAKE. You've gotta promise to forget it as soon as I tell you.

MOLLY. Okay.

JAKE. When your mother and I were on our honeymoon, we went to the State Fair and had an authentic gypsy woman read our palms. She read Maggie's and then mine. Without saying a word. We waited. Then she said, "Sky and Earth and finally Water. You, my friend, will be the Third." (*Pause.*) We asked her several times which one of us she was talking to. She wouldn't say. I offered her a buck. She wouldn't say. To this day, I'm not sure if that prophecy belongs to Maggie or me – but when I look at these two graves and hear "You, my friend, will be the Third," I get more than a little bit of a chill.

MOLLY. How come you never told me this before?

JAKE. 'Fraid you'd think someone else was bowling my frame.

MOLLY. Shouldn't you pray or something?

(*JAKE whirls and heads back to his chair, driving DYSON back into The Shadows.*)

JAKE. Oh, they'd love that. WHOEVER KNOWS THINGS would love me to close my eyes and pray so they could sneak up on me – (*Grabs* Reader's Digest.) But I'm gonna sit right here with "Life in these United States" and keep a lookout. (*Dives into his* Reader's Digest.)

MOLLY. It's May thirteenth, you know.

JAKE. (*As HE reads.*) Yeah. Gotta order pencils.

MOLLY. This is their birthday. How old would they be?

JAKE. Who? Lois or Loretta?

MOLLY. Both of them.

JAKE. They had the same birthday?

MOLLY. Yeah. Don't you remember?

JAKE. I think they did that just to piss me off.

MOLLY. Different years. Same day. Makes it easy to remember.

JAKE. For you it does. You're still pretty fresh off the woodpile, girl. I been in the fire awhile.

MOLLY. Figured out which is which, yet?

JAKE. Go down and sweep the lanes, okay?

MOLLY. Already did.

JAKE. Shine the balls.

MOLLY. Done.

JAKE. Sharpen the pencils, empty the ashtrays, dust the trophy.

MOLLY. The trophy gives me the creeps.

JAKE. Why?

MOLLY. Ever since Lois died, you know?

JAKE. Yeah, but you still gotta dust it.

MOLLY. I polished it, too. (*Pause.*) Want me to tell you which is which?

JAKE. No. (*Pause.*) I already know. Don't waste your breath. I buried both of them myself, didn't I? I oughtta know.

MOLLY. Why didn't you mark the graves?

JAKE. I was gonna, but by the time I got around to it, I'd –

MOLLY. Forgotten.

JAKE. *Decided against it.*

MOLLY. Tell me then. (*Pause.*) C'mon. (*Pause.*) You don't know.

JAKE. I'm narrowing it down.

MOLLY. Why don't you dig 'em up? Then you'd know. (*Pause.*) What's the big deal? They're dead. Dead is dead.

JAKE. Molly, do you know what you're saying? You're talking about your moms here.

MOLLY. My stepmoms.

JAKE. Whatever.

MOLLY. You wouldn't catch *my* mom up here.

JAKE. Maggie was allergic to dirt. They'll cremate her.

MOLLY. Will they give me the ashes?

JAKE. I don't think so. You've got the bike, Molly.

MOLLY. I want the ashes. Can we go get them?

JAKE. Molly, if we were ever able – after all these years – to find Maggie, I would hope we'd find more than just her ashes.

MOLLY. You loved her.

JAKE. Not a bit.

MOLLY. You loved her. I know you did. You cried when she left.

JAKE. Goddamn allergies.

MOLLY. Did you love her more than Lois and Loretta?

JAKE. (*Leads her away from the graves a bit, talks softer, but intensely.*) Molly. Soon – maybe three words from now – WHOEVER KNOWS THINGS is gonna find a way to kill me. And when that happens, I have to spend all of eternity with these women. I am not going to say something that will haunt me for the rest of my death. That's also why I am not going to dig them up to find out which is which. They are content where they are and I'm content that someday I'll remember. We are family members, not archaeologists.

MOLLY. Whenever you want to know, just ask.

(*JAKE tries to ignore her by burying himself in his* Reader's Digest. *MOLLY spins the pinwheels.*)

MOLLY. (*Sings.*)
No one here can love or understand me
Oh what hard luck stories they all hand me

(*To audience.*)

We're gonna be alone any minute now. Dad used to have insomnia until a few months ago when I bought him the subscription. (*Sings, like a lullaby.*)
Make my bed and light the light
I'll be home late tonight
Blackbird Bye Bye

(*JAKE's head slumps forward. HE is dead asleep.*)

MOLLY. Works like a charm. (*Goes to her bike and unlocks the chain and wraps it up during the following.*) My mom's name is Maggie. Wife number one. Very beautiful. Very rich. She met Dad when he was on his way to the Wyoming Conservatory of Music. Their eyes met in the train station. She going northeast, he southwest. They held their gaze as their trains departed – leaving them standing on opposite platforms. She in her silk dress and high heels, he in his overalls and feed cap. She liked his style. They went in a bar with an adjacent bowling alley. These were the days of pin setters — young kids who set the pins by hand after each ball. Two hours later they were run out of that alley because my dad threw a bowling ball so hard and sprayed pins so far that none of those boys would stand back there and set 'em. She liked his style. Dad bought his first pair of dark socks and the marriage was held in New York City. They acquired a house and a car and a business with Maggie's money. She threw a lot of parties. Dad bought his first necktie and worked a twenty-hour week behind a desk, and made more in one month than this daddy had made on the farm in one year. They had a daughter and named her Molly and when she was ten, Dad found a new bicycle in the front hall with an envelope taped to the handlebars. Inside the envelope was five thousand dollars and my birth certificate. Maggie was gone. Dad brought us back here where he grew up and bought this piece of land which included the only bowling alley in town. He worked the counter and I set the pins till we got automated. Then I worked the counter with Lois, who was wife number two till she died. Then I worked the counter with Loretta, who was wife number three till she died. Now, I work the counter alone and Dad tries not to get married.

(*MOLLY places the third pinwheel in Jake's lap and kisses him on the forehead. SHE steps back and looks at all three pinwheels. A BREEZE comes up and they begin to turn.*)

MOLLY. (*Sings.*)
Happy Birthday to you,
Happy Birthday to you,
Happy Birthday dear Lois ... (*Indicates Stage Right grave.*)
and Loretta ... (*Indicates Stage Left grave.*)
Happy Birthday to you. (*Mounts her bike.*)
Neither of them liked his style, but they loved him just the same.

(*MOLLY rides off on her bike as the BREEZE subsides and the pinwheels stop turning.*
DYSON appears from The Shadows, watches Molly leave, then approaches Jake slowly from behind as HE speaks.)

DYSON. I am good at what I do. I always get what I go after. There is no way at this time that Mister Tomlinson will be able to escape me. The situation is somewhat akin to that of a vintage Thunderbird with mags and headers pursuing a 1967 Rambler. The Bird will toy with the Rambler for a few blocks ... and then gun it. (*Stopped by the sound of a woman's voice, singing.*) That is all I can say to you now.

(*LORETTA enters, singing. SHE carries three clay pots of geraniums and a small trowel. The pinwheel at the head of her grave begins to turn. The other pinwheels do not move. SHE walks very near Mister Dyson, but is not aware of his presence. DYSON is frozen with confusion.*)

LORETTA. (*Singing.*)
Pack up all my care and woe
Here I go singin' low
Bye Bye Blackbird

Where somebody waits for me
Sugar's sweet and so is he
Bye Bye Blackbird

(*LORETTA takes Jake's shovel and rake and smoothes her grave into a nice, flat patch of dirt. Then SHE begins to plant the geraniums. SHE speaks to the audience as she does this. DYSON watches from a distance, mesmerized.*)

LORETTA. (*To audience.*) Lois was my best friend. I was her maid of honor when she married Jake. Even though it was his second time, it was her first, so she wore white and a veil, and Jake still had his dark socks so they saved a little money there. She knew she was getting used merchandise, but she loved him anyway. Now he's twice-used merchandise. Might be damaged for all I know. (*SHE walks over to Lois grave.*) I helped him bury her. We waited till Monday cause that's the day the alley is closed. The moon was still out and the sun was just coming up and Jake and Molly and I sang "Bye Bye Blackbird" cause that was her favorite. Jake buried her with her custom-made turquoise-speckled Voit bowling ball. That's the first time I ever saw him cry and he said "goddamn allergies" and walked down this hill to the alley and threw balls at pins as hard as he could – overhand sometimes – until sundown, and then he fell asleep on lane number four, leaving a seven-ten split still standing. He didn't talk for twelve days and when he finally did, the first thing out of his mouth was –

JAKE. (*Suddenly very awake.*) I HATE THAT GODDAMN ALLEY, LORETTA.

(*JAKE's outburst sends DYSON back into The Shadows.*)

LORETTA. I know you do.

JAKE. It makes me think of meeting Maggie and how I never got to Wyoming and how she left me and Molly with a personal check and a brand new Schwinn and that pisses me off. And now every time I hear a ball smash into a pin I think of how you introduced me to Lois at the alley and how I gave her some pointers and how she broke forty for the first time on her way to a 256 which helped us win the annual Turtle Rapids/Mudler Bowl-Off and how I told her she could carry home the trophy only seconds before lightning hit it and killed her. I HATE THAT GODDAMN ALLEY, LORETTA.

LORETTA. I know you do. (*Silence. LORETTA returns to her geraniums and works. JAKE walks up and stands very near her. SHE hands him a rake. HE rakes the patch of dirt that he rose from into a nice, flat patch of earth. The following dialogue underscores this.*)

JAKE. Looks awful nice, Loretta.

LORETTA. She loved geraniums.

JAKE. Hated roses, though.

LORETTA. No, she liked roses. These'll last longer.

JAKE. That's right. *You* hate roses.

LORETTA. No.

JAKE. Who the hell hates roses, then?

LORETTA. No one I know.

KNIGHT. Someone does.

LORETTA. I'll bring some more up tomorrow and fill in that patch you're raking there.

(*LORETTA stands and discovers JAKE standing very near her, staring at her. Pause.*)

LORETTA. You doin' okay, Jake?

JAKE. Hell, I'm fine.

LORETTA. Molly says you never sleep anymore.

JAKE. I'm fine. I'm beyond fine. I'm damn near to great. I'm from good stock, I got my health, I got my teeth, I got a case of Fresca at home – I got all I need. (*Pause.*) You want to get married, Loretta? (*Very long silence.*)

LORETTA. To who?

JAKE. To who do you think? I got a great kid, a good house, a nice business and you'd only have to work the counter three days a week. I promise not to make you carry the trophy outside during a storm. (*Pause.*) I like you, Loretta. Always have. From the first glance you ever gave me.

LORETTA. You love me?

JAKE. I *really* like you.

LORETTA. I don't want a man who doesn't love me.

JAKE. Quote me, Loretta – love is serious.

LORETTA. So am I.

(*JAKE sets up the lawn chair a little too near Lois' grave.*)

JAKE. Sit down, will you, Loretta? (*Softens.*) Please.

(*SHE does.*)

JAKE. Now, look. Love is a very big thing. It's an overwhelming condition. Like being too drunk to go bowling. It just doesn't happen very often. (*Pause.*) Do you understand what I'm sayin'?

LORETTA. Yes.

JAKE. Good.

LORETTA. And my answer is *no*.

JAKE. Now, wait. Love is also something you shoot for. Love is the three-hundred game, Loretta. It's twelve strikes straight to the heart and when it happens there's nothing left standing. (*Pause.*) Do you see that?

LORETTA. Yes.

JAKE. Good.

LORETTA. And if this isn't that, then my answer to you is *no*.

JAKE. Damnit, Loretta, I've bowled three hundred twice now in my life and I lost both times. I can't do it again.

(*LORETTA stands and walks to the other side of Lois's grave so that it is between them.*)

LORETTA. How long were you married to Maggie?

JAKE. Fourteen years.

LORETTA. And how long after she left did you marry Lois?

JAKE. Four years.

LORETTA. And how long were you married to Lois?

JAKE. One year.

LORETTA. And how long has it been since the funeral?

JAKE. Twelve days.

LORETTA. You're getting pretty good at this, Jake. Soon, you'll have it down to marriages and funerals on alternate days.

JAKE. Loretta, look —

LORETTA. You haven't even put the headstone on!

JAKE. I will. I'm getting to it. Just listen. I *really, really* like you, Loretta. And at my age, that's so damn close to love that I could hit it from here with a rock. (*Pause.*) Think about it, will you? (*Pause, smiles.*) I already got my suit and everything.

LORETTA. (*Smiles and throws a dirt clod at him.*) Get out of here.

MOLLY. (*Enters quickly on her bike.*) Hey, Dad!

JAKE. What?

MOLLY. Oh, hi, Loretta.

LORETTA. Hi, Molly. How's things?

MOLLY. We got problems. Dad, the pin machine's gone haywire and the ball return is broken. People are rolling all sorts of stuff down the lanes to hit the pins.

JAKE. What sort of stuff?

MOLLY. Like cats and stuff.

JAKE. Goddamned automated pin machines! Should never have bought one I told you that, Molly. In my day, we didn't have 'em. We had kids that worked for a sandwich and a coke and never broke down. And now here we are with –

MOLLY. Yeah, Dad. I know. You better get down there.

JAKE. Yeah.

MOLLY. Want my bike?

JAKE. Uh ... (*Looks at Loretta.*) No. I mean, yeah. Sure. (*To Molly.*) I'm goin'. (*Loretta, from bike.*) Uh ... *real, real* nice flowers, Loretta.

LORETTA. Bye, Jake.

(*JAKE rides down the hill out of sight.*)

MOLLY. He thinks pin setters are romantic cause he never had to set pins. I did. (*Starts to go down the hill.*)

LORETTA. Molly?

MOLLY. Yeah?

LORETTA. Do you remember when your dad and Lois got married?

MOLLY. Sure.

LORETTA. What did you think about that?

MOLLY. What do you mean?

LORETTA. Did you like her?

MOLLY. Yeah.

LORETTA. Do you miss her?

MOLLY. He asked you, didn't he? I told him to wait. I told him to wait at least three weeks or you'd think he was just on the rebound from Lois and figured that since you two were such good friends that you could take her place when in fact, for all he knows, you might be better than she ever was. He asked you, didn't he?

LORETTA. Yes. He did.

MOLLY. I knew it. (*Pause.*) What're you gonna do?

LORETTA. I'm not sure. You know him better than I do. What would you do?

MOLLY. If I were you?

LORETTA. Yes.

MOLLY. You really want to know?

LORETTA. Yes.

MOLLY. Well ... it gets a little boring in the afternoon, but you'll have weekends off and you'll get free lane time if no one's waiting. (*Pause.*) Lois never used the free lane time. (*Pause.*) You okay, Loretta? (*Silence.*)

LORETTA. He didn't ask me to work for him, Molly.

MOLLY. He didn't?

LORETTA. No.

MOLLY. Well ... don't worry. He will. Give it another week or so.

LORETTA. He asked me to marry him.

(*Silence.*)

MOLLY. Wow.

LORETTA. Yeah. Wow. (*Silence.*)

MOLLY. Well ... there's a couple things I've got to tell you. Don't let Dad tell you a big sob story about Louie Twinkler and the Wyoming

Conservatory of Music. Lois believed him. But it was love. Pure and simple. He won't admit it, but it was love.

LORETTA. Okay.

MOLLY. Don't ever get rid of my bike. Even if I leave home. Hold onto it for me.

LORETTA. All right.

MOLLY. And, at the reception, no matter how much he begs and pleads and even if he offers you a custom-made Voit with your initials on it, *do not* let him put Fresca in the punch bowl. I could've killed him last time he did that.

LORETTA. (*Laughs. Pause.*) Molly, do you know that I'm only ten years older than you?

MOLLY. Small town's gotta have something to talk about. Want me to call you "Mom?"

LORETTA. I haven't said yes, yet, Molly.

MOLLY. I called Lois, "Mom." She liked that. (*Pause.*) You miss her? (*Pause.*) She was your best friend, huh?

LORETTA. (*Looking at Lois' grave.*) Yeah. (*Pause.*)

MOLLY. I'll be your best friend, if you want.

(*Pause. THEY hug.*)

MOLLY. You gonna leave?

LORETTA. Now?

MOLLY. If you get married. Gonna leave Turtle Rapids?

LORETTA. Wouldn't think so.

MOLLY. Why not?

LORETTA. This is home.

MOLLY. Don't you ever wonder what people look like in South Carolina?

LORETTA. No. I guess I don't.

MOLLY. I wonder about that.

LORETTA. A lot?

MOLLY. A lot. Not just that. Other things. Huge bodies of water. Skyscrapers. Who lives in Utah and why?

LORETTA. You got nothin' but time, Molly.

(*THEY sit. LORETTA strokes Molly's hair.*)

MOLLY. Hey, Loretta?

LORETTA. Yeah?

MOLLY. Know what else?

LORETTA. What?

MOLLY. I wonder what's inside me. You know?

LORETTA. Yeah. I know.

MOLLY. I want to be able to ask my mom that. Just once. Am I going to be smart or stupid or tall or pretty or boring or what? Are people gonna ask me to dance? Am I going to learn the piano or run a marathon or do brain surgery or meet a chimney sweep or go back East and sell Lava Lamps?

LORETTA. I don't know, Molly.

MOLLY. I think my mom'd know. If she were here. Don't you think she'd know?

LORETTA. (*Pause.*) She might.

MOLLY. You'd liked my mom.

LORETTA. Yeah?

MOLLY. Yeah. She's left-handed like you.

(*THEY laugh. MOLLY stands.*)

MOLLY. Well, I better go see if he's kicked the machine enough to fix it. Want to walk down with me?

LORETTA. Not just yet.

MOLLY. (*Pause.*) Hey, Loretta?

LORETTA. Yeah?

MOLLY. Do it. He's a good guy.

LORETTA. Thanks, Molly.

MOLLY. No sweat. Welcome aboard. (*Goes down the hill, leaving Loretta alone.*)

LORETTA. (*Sits and speaks to the audience.*) My thoughts that night were about yellow lights. Yellow traffic lights.

(*DYSON pokes his head out of The Shadows.*)

LORETTA. There is that imperceptible distance at which our mind tells us we can beat the red light. Some stranger inside that keeps us from slamming on the brakes. (*Pause.*) I didn't stop. I bought a new dress. I set my hair. And I gunned it.

(*DYSON returns to The Shadows.*)

LORETTA. Pastor Sodderburger married us and we had champagne and cake and moonlight bowling at the reception. I kept my job at the Bee Hive in the mornings and worked the counter at the Dust Bowl in the afternoons. A lot of people come to the Bee Hive 'cause I'm there to give them a cut or a perm. I didn't want to leave them all to Doris. Doris is my partner. Doris doesn't quite understand that she only as to look at their hair for a couple hours – but they've got to wear it to church on Sunday. Her customers seldom leave through the front door. I'm a good hairdresser because I tell the truth. I mean, I'm polite about it – I don't say "You are remarkably ugly and no hairstyle in the world could ever save you." But I do tell them what I think. Ugly people are not the problem. The hardest part of my job is people who come in looking beautiful, truly beautiful – and want to leave looking *better*. That happened to me the other day. A new face – and we don't get a lot of those – came moseying into the Bee Hive and asked what I could do with her hair. I said, "Lady, I could shave your head and you'd still be ravishing." (*Pause.*) I had no way of knowing it was Maggie.

(*JAKE comes running up the hill. Stops suddenly when he sees Loretta. Long silence.*)

LORETTA. She looked great.

JAKE. I wasn't gonna ask.

LORETTA. Sure you were. (*Pause.*) She took all my conversation, Jake. I babbled on about you and Molly and the Dust Bowl and I never knew it was her until two hours later when the man she was with put down his paper and said, "You ready to go, Maggie?" And she looked me in the eye and touched her hair and she said, "Yes. I think I am." Off they went, leaving me with a chair full of red hair and a fifty dollar tip.

JAKE. (*Pause. Tentatively.*) What did the, uh – was he – ?

LORETTA. You really want to know?

JAKE. No. (*Pause.*) Yeah.

LORETTA. He was tall. But not too tall. Handsome. Smoked a pipe. Read the *Wall Street Journal.*

JAKE. Ever picked up mule ears?

LORETTA. What?

JAKE. Seven-ten split. You know.

LORETTA. Oh. (*Smiles.*) I didn't ask.

JAKE. Bet he hasn't. Bet he doesn't even own shoes. Rents 'em. The guy's a loser. (*Pause.*) They go see Molly?

LORETTA. She had me give her chauffeur directions to the high school, but when I looked out the window, they were heading north.

JAKE. She say where they were comin' from?

LORETTA. Sydney.

JAKE. Huh. Didn't know she knew any folks in Nebraska.

LORETTA. Australia. Sydney. Australia. (*Silence.*) Are you running this alley cause it reminds you of Maggie?

JAKE. I am running this alley because of a man named Louie Twinkler. Because of him, I got Conway Twitty on the jukebox instead of Chopin in my fingers. Because of that goddamn good-for-nothing Louie Twinkler, I never –

LORETTA. Jake.

JAKE. What?

LORETTA. Save the story.

JAKE. Those years are goners, Loretta. I don't want 'em back.

LORETTA. You came runnin' up here awful fast when you heard she'd been to the shop.

JAKE. I was in the middle of fixin' the ball rack – couple nails left to pound – when Doris called and told me Maggie'd been there. I ran to the Bee Hive to see –

LORETTA. *Who?*

JAKE. *You* (*Pause.*) Doris told me you were up here. (*Pause.*) I gotta ask you something, Loretta. (*Pause.*) Does Doris *know* her hair is purple?

LORETTA. (*Smiles.*) I gotta go to my second job, now. My boss is a slave driver.

JAKE. No, you don't.

LORETTA. Who's working the counter?

JAKE. Put 'er on automatic pilot. Look, I'm thinkin' your boss should let you off early to drive up to Gleason and get some barbecued chicken.

LORETTA. You got your eye on my fifty dollar tip, don't you?

JAKE. Six-thirty. I'll be the guy in the Rambler.

LORETTA. What about Family Night?

JAKE. Have the last person out unplug the sign. (*He kisses her.*) I damn near almost love you, Loretta.

LORETTA. Then get that ball rack fixed before it falls on someone's head.

JAKE. Don't you worry.

(*THEY kiss.*)

LORETTA. See you.

(*LORETTA exits down the hill. LIGHTS have shifted to late afternoon.*)

JAKE. (*Gathers up the tools as he speaks. To audience.*) That woman can make a loaf of bread that smells so good you think you've sinned. I can storm home from the alley, in a rage about something or another, and when I reach for that back screen door and smell that smell – I become *stupid.* That bread seeks out taste buds you killed years ago with three-two beer and brings them back to life. (*Pause.*) My momma used to make bread like that and send me to school with sandwiches. Big, thick slices with a hard brown crust. And all the city kids had *Wonder Bread* which was soft and sliced thin and was a sign that they had less dirt under their nails than me. And I would trade my momma's sandwiches every day with Mikey Swanson so I could get that *Wonder Bread* and feel like a city kid on top of the world. And I'd beg my momma to buy some Wonder Bread so the kids at school wouldn't laugh at me. And one time the grocer was out of flour and Dad brought home a loaf of *Wonder Bread* and my momma made me a sandwich and I took it to school and Mikey Swanson never talked to me again. (*Pause.*) Someone who can make a good loaf of bread knows some secrets about the universe.

(*MOLLY comes running up the hill, out of breath, frantic.*)

JAKE. What is it, kiddo?
MOLLY. We had an accident.
JAKE. What kind of accident?
MOLLY. The ball rack.
JAKE. What?
MOLLY. *Fell.*
JAKE. Ah, damn.
MOLLY. On top of Loretta.

(*JAKE stares at Molly in disbelief. SHE grabs his arm.*)

MOLLY. You better come.

(JAKE drops the tools and the TWO OF THEM run off down the hill.
DYSON bolts out of The Shadows, looking as though he may follow them – but stops when HE hears SINGING behind him.
The pinwheel at the head of Lois' grave begins to SPIN.
LOIS appears, carrying three clay pots of geraniums, and walks to her grave.
DYSON watches her, baffled. SHE is not aware of him.
SHE sets the pots down, grabs the tools and levels out her grave as SHE sings. When it is a nice level piece of earth, SHE plants the geraniums there.)

   LOIS. *(Singing.)*
Where somebody waits for me
Sugar's sweet and so is he
Bye Bye Blackbird

No one here can love or understand me
Oh what hard luck stories they all –

(Turns and sees audience.)

   LOIS. Can you believe it? I married a guy that runs a bowling alley. I wait thirty years for an astrophysicist and then settle for a guy with a nice personality. Must've lost my edge somewhere

along the line. It's hard in a place like this to keep
your standards high. My friend, Norma, got
married last year and when Jimmy Ray got home
from the courthouse with their license, it turned
out to be a hunting license. Big game. She said to
me, "Lois, can you believe they'd make a mistake
like that?" I said I thought that summed up Jimmy
Ray pretty well. (*Pause.*) My friend Loretta
introduced me to Jake. He bought me a Fresca at
the alley. We drove up to Gleason and walked
along the lake. Then, I didn't see him for two
weeks.

(*LOIS' pinwheel STOPS SPINNING.*
JAKE enters with a Fresca. HE is a little gussied
up – maybe a clean shirt and hair a bit too
combed. HE takes off his Dust Bowl cap when
he sees Lois. Pause.)

JAKE. Hey, there.
LOIS. Somebody die?
JAKE. What?
LOIS. The shirt.
JAKE. Huh? Oh ... no. Sometimes the clean
ones make it to the top of the drawer.
LOIS. Thought you'd fallen off the earth or
something.
JAKE. Damn near.
LOIS. Yeah.
JAKE. Yeah. Went to Wyoming.
LOIS. Just for fun?

JAKE. I had a bridge to burn. Some twenty-two years I've carried around this picture in my head of the Wyoming Conservatory of Music. Kept imagining these ivy-covered mansions with kids readin' thick books on the stairs. Little bits of song comin' out of fourth floor windows. Young women with old cellos. Some kind of damn never-never-land.

LOIS. Sounds beautiful.

JAKE. I met the president of the Conservatory during a break from his mail route, and he showed me the one-story building with aluminum siding that sits across the road from the sewage treatment plant.

LOIS. Why'd you finally decide to go look at it?

JAKE. Made the mistake of gettin' married to Maggie before I'd given that place a shot. Regretted doin' that, Lois. WHOEVER KNOWS THINGS told me to have a look and get it out of my system. I didn't want to think about gettin' married again till I'd seen what I was missing.

LOIS. Married?

JAKE. (*Behind the lawn chair.*) Sit down, will you Lois?

(*Pause. LOIS sits in the chair. Pause.*)

JAKE. Fresca?
LOIS. No.

(*SHE takes it from him, however, and puts it on the ground. HE walks away a bit.*)

JAKE. Lois, do you remember when we were up at Gleason two weeks ago?

LOIS. Yes.

JAKE. Walkin' around the lake up there?

LOIS. Yes.

JAKE. And we stopped by those twin maples and skipped some stones?

LOIS. Mmm-hmmm.

JAKE. I looked at you and do you remember what I said?

LOIS. (*After a moment.*) You didn't say anything.

JAKE. (*Very excited.*) See, you remember it, too!

LOIS. Remember what? Nothing happened.

JAKE. Plenty happened. I watched a damn Roman candle go off in my brain.

LOIS. What?

JAKE. *Fireworks,* Lois.

LOIS. (*Pause.*) I think you better start over.

(*MOLLY races in on her bike; SHE has overheard the preceding.*)

MOLLY. Yeah, Dad. Start over.

JAKE. Molly —

MOLLY. No way. I wouldn't miss this for the world.

JAKE. (*Pause.*) Where was I at?

LOIS. Fireworks.

JAKE. Yeah, right. Well. See. Thing is, Lois, that I hadn't seen 'em in a long while and there we were walking around Moby Lake up at Gleason where my dad drowned because he stopped to think about walkin' on the water and looked down instead of just tryin' to get to the other side and it dawned on what's left of my brain that I could stop and think about why I was seein' fireworks when you smiled at me – or I could just go on ahead and see how far it'd carry me.

LOIS. How far *what* will carry you?

JAKE. This feeling I got.

LOIS. What's the feeling?

JAKE. Can't describe it.

LOIS. Sure you can.

JAKE. No.

LOIS. C'mon, Jake.

JAKE. No.

MOLLY. C'mon, Dad.

JAKE. (*To Molly.*) You stay out of this.

LOIS. (*To Jake.*) Try. (*Pause.*)

JAKE. Well ... it's a feeling like when I first got my reading glasses and everything on the page was the same as it had been the day before, but the blur was gone. (*Pause.*) That sort of feeling. (*Silence.*)

LOIS. (*Smiles.*) What do you think, Molly? Should we give him another shot?

MOLLY. I don't know. Think it'll get any better?

LOIS. Hard to say.

JAKE. I don't need this from you two, I'll tell you twice.

MOLLY. Lighten up, Dad.

JAKE. It didn't come out like I rehearsed it.

MOLLY. (*To Lois.*) I told you.

LOIS. You rehearsed it, did you?

JAKE. It's a long ride back from Wyoming.

MOLLY. Your turn, Lois.

JAKE. What?

MOLLY. We had two weeks to rehearse, too, you know.

JAKE. How did you know that I –

MOLLY. She knew, Dad.

JAKE. Lois –

LOIS. Yeah. I knew.

JAKE. (*Pause.*) Well?

LOIS. Sit down, will you Jake?

(*HE does. Pause.*)

LOIS. Jake, do you remember when Loretta introduced us?

JAKE. Like it was this morning.

LOIS. Well, right before she did that, she took me aside and told me you were the kind of man that needed his pockets gone through. I asked her why on earth I'd care what you had in your pockets and she said not his pants, kiddo, his *heart*. Make sure he's not hidin' something down in there where he'll never let you get at it. Make sure you're not competin' for space. (*Pause.*) So, that's what I'm askin' you, Jake.

(*Silence.*)

JAKE. I can't tell you I've forgotten Maggie, cause the best part of Maggie's still around. (*Looks at Molly.*) She's standin' right there watchin' her old man sweat. And I can't tell you that I've forgotten some of the things she taught me. Like to use the short fork for salad. And that I was strong enough to raise my daughter without her. (*Pause, points to heart.*) But hell, Lois, I got pockets in here that ain't never held a dime.

(*LOIS walks to Jake, HE stands and faces her.*)

MOLLY. Want me to leave?

(*THEY do not look at Molly. LOIS takes Jake's head in her hands and kisses him passionately.*)

LOIS. What are you thinking?
JAKE. I'm tryin' not to.
LOIS. Why?
JAKE. 'Fraid I'd think it was unbelievable and then sink.

(*THEY kiss.*)

JAKE. (*Staring at Lois.*) Molly, what time is
it?
MOLLY. Almost five.

(*THEY kiss.*)

JAKE. (*Still staring at Lois.*) Molly, what day
is it?
MOLLY. Wednesday.

(*THEY kiss.*)

JAKE. (*Still staring at Lois.*) Molly –
MOLLY. Yeah, Dad. *Hawaiian Night. Five
minutes.*
JAKE. I ask for a kid, I get an alarm clock.

(*MOLLY mounts her bike. JAKE pulls away from
Lois. SHE hands him his Fresca.*)

JAKE. Soon?
LOIS. Yeah.

(*JAKE goes down the hill. Brief pause.*)

MOLLY. You gonna stay here?
LOIS. When?
MOLLY. When you're married?
LOIS. Sure we are.

MOLLY. Why?

LOIS. This is home.

MOLLY. Don't you ever wonder what they eat in Brooklyn?

LOIS. (*After a moment.*) I guess I don't.

MOLLY. I do. And other stuff. Boys.

LOIS. (*Smiles.*) Boys, huh?

MOLLY. Yeah.

LOIS. What about 'em?

MOLLY. Where are they all?

LOIS. They're out there.

MOLLY. What good are they?

LOIS. Not much. But every so often you get lucky.

MOLLY. How do you mean?

LOIS. You find someone you didn't expect.

MOLLY. Like a steal?

LOIS. (*Baffled.*) What's that?

MOLLY. When you get more pins than you should with the ball you threw.

LOIS. Uh, yeah. I guess. Boys talk a good lick, see?

MOLLY. Like bench work.

LOIS. Huh?

MOLLY. Inside stuff. Patter. Make the other team choke.

LOIS. Right. They hang out in little groups.

MOLLY. Dinner bucket. Granny's teeth.

LOIS. Some of those boys know their stuff.

MOLLY. Gettin' good wood.

LOIS. Others are a little off.

MOLLY. Dodo ball.

LOIS. But more often than not, it's the one standing alone in the corner ...

MOLLY. Lone maple.

LOIS. ... That'll turn out to be the real catch.

MOLLY. (*Understanding.*) Like pickin' a cherry to make that mark.

LOIS. (*Pause. Looks at Molly. Smiles.*) Whatever you say, Molly.

MOLLY. You know, you're pretty fun to talk to, Lois.

LOIS. Well, I think you know more about bowling than I've ever known about boys. (*Pause.*) You people really say those things?

MOLLY. Sure. It's a language.

LOIS. Molly, I don't think boys are gonna be a problem at all.

(*Silence.*)

MOLLY. (*Saying it for the first time.*) Hey, *Mom.*

LOIS. (*Smiles.*) Yeah?

MOLLY. Think you'll like bein' my mom?

LOIS. A lot. (*Pause.*)

MOLLY. Would you come visit me?

(*LOIS looks at her.*)

MOLLY. If I was far away?

LOIS. You bet I would.

MOLLY. Singapore?

LOIS. Yep.

MOLLY. Utah?

LOIS. Yep.

MOLLY. Duck Hollow?

LOIS. No.

MOLLY. (*Laughs.*) Why not?

LOIS. If you don't cross a state line, Molly, it just doesn't count.

MOLLY. I wish I wasn't sixteen.

LOIS. Talk to me when you're thirty. Molly, you got nothin' but time.

MOLLY. Yeah. (*Pause.*) 'Cept I'm late for Hawaiian Night. You wanna come slam ten?

LOIS. What?

(*MOLLY rolls an invisible ball.*)

LOIS. Oh, I don't know, Molly ...

MOLLY. Dad bought Don Ho records.

LOIS. I think I'll pass.

(*MOLLY rides her bike off down the hill.*)

LOIS. (*Turns to the audience and pulls up a chair.*) Bowling, to me, is something you do if you're given a choice between bowling and death. And even then it's a toss-up. Jake calls it the last of the "never-too" sports. You're never too old or too tired or too poor or too drunk or too stupid to go bowling. It's kind of the Campbell's Tomato Soup

of sports. Don't get me wrong. I like working at
the Dust Bowl. I like the people. But I have no
desire to put on slippery shoes, lift a heavy object,
and knock down things that have been carefully
arranged. It's not exhilarating like darts or
horseshoes. I wouldn't be surprised if death is
more fun than bowling.

JAKE. (*Comes running up the hill, out of
breath.*) LOIS! (*Sees her.*) Lois, have you seen
Sidney?

LOIS. You mean Pastor Sodderburger?

JAKE. Yeah. You seen him?

LOIS. No.

JAKE. We bowl against Mudler in two hours
and if Sidney isn't there we're gonna get killed
and lose the trophy.

LOIS. I didn't know he was on the team.

JAKE. Lois, he *is* the team. He bowls a 195 and
can time a prayer to coincide with the exact
moment any ball hits any pin. He raises
everyone's average thirty points just by being
there. Lois, without him, we're goners.

LOIS. Surely someone can take his place.

JAKE. *God* could not take his place.

LOIS. You're making Loretta bowl on the
night of her birthday?

JAKE. Tonight's her birthday?

LOIS. Yep.

JAKE. Can't be. You said her birthday was the
same as yours.

LOIS. You got it.

(*Silence.*)

JAKE. Oh. (*Goes to her and kisses her on the forehead.*) Happy Birthday, Lois.

LOIS. Thanks so much.

JAKE. Look. We can celebrate Thursday, okay?

LOIS. Thursday's Elvis Night.

JAKE. We'll cancel it. I'll take the records back. Lois. I've waited all year to win back this trophy. It's a pride thing, you know?

LOIS. It's a trophy. That's all it is. And it's an *ugly* trophy.

JAKE. (*Exasperated.*) Lois. I look at you sometimes and wonder how I ever fell in love with a non-bowler. It's not just a trophy. It is the symbol of the annual Turtle Rapids/Mudler Bowl-Off. We held the trophy since I bought the alley until last year when we lost it on account of Mudler recruiting college kids from Duck Hollow. And they'll kill us again this year – don't think they won't – and they'll go home with that trophy again, unless I can find Sidney and –

LOIS. Pastor Sodderburger.

JAKE. – And get him on our side so that God will be on our side. Now, help me find him, will you?

LOIS. Jake, I don't get it. I never will. A man starts out to be a world renowned piano player and ends up a small town bowling nut.

JAKE. It's a long story, Lois. I don't have time.

LOIS. Is it about Maggie?

JAKE. No.

LOIS. You can tell me, you know.

JAKE. IT'S NOT ABOUT MAGGIE. Why do you always think everything's about Maggie? I never talk about her.

LOIS. Exactly. An occasional mention of her name would make me feel great. It would let me know you're not holding her so tight inside that there's no room for me.

JAKE. I gotta go, Lois –

LOIS. Molly said you quit music because of Maggie.

JAKE. LOIS –

LOIS. You won her heart at a bowling alley and you've been trying to get it back ever since. Is that true?

JAKE. No.

LOIS. Then what is it?

JAKE. Lois –

LOIS. I want the truth.

(*Silence.*)

JAKE. Louie Twinkler.

LOIS. (*After a moment.*) *Who?*

JAKE. Louie Twinkler. He played shortstop for Mudler twenty-some years ago when they were playin' our own Turtle Rapids Rabbits for the county baseball championship. It was three days before I was leaving for the Wyoming Conservatory of Music. I'd been pounding the cardboard for six hours a day.

LOIS. You mean the *keyboard.*

JAKE. Cardboard, Lois. Mom and Dad couldn't afford a real piano, but they were determined that I play. So, Dad made me a cardboard keyboard and painted little black and white keys on it, and Mom bought me a book and said "Learn the *fingering*, son. That's the hard part." So, I'd play silent scales and original compositions for six hours a day, and Dad would come in from the fields and say "Sounds real good, Jake. Is that a new one?"

LOIS. Jake, are you —

JAKE. Quote me, Lois. So, there I was, three days away from playing a real piano — when I dove from my seat to grab a foul ball down the first base line off the bat of Louie Twinkler. (*Pause.*) People three rows back heard the bones pop. That foul ball gnarled my hand something awful. Twinkler struck out on the next pitch out of shame. But so much for Wyoming and so much for my future until I discovered that the Twinkler foul ball had created ... a perfectly constructed bowling hand. A custom-made injury. A gnarled masterpiece. I chucked the cardboard and hit the lanes. (*Pause.*) It was Louie, Lois. Not Maggie. Now, what do you think of that?

(*Silence.*)

    LOIS. (*Stares at him.*) He's in Duck Hollow.
    JAKE. What?
    LOIS. Pastor Sodderburger. He's giving the commencement speech at the Vo Tech School of Bartending. He'll be back tomorrow.
    JAKE. (*Suspiciously.*) Duck Hollow?
    LOIS. Yeah.
    JAKE. Pray that I catch him before he leaves!

(*JAKE races off. LOIS finishes weeding the flower patch and speaks to the audience.*)

    LOIS. It's a fine line between a storyteller and a liar. I try to believe the storyteller and ignore the liar for fear they'll both go away. (*Works the flower bed, humming "Bye Bye Blackbird" softly, to herself.*)

(*DYSON appears from The Shadows and moves towards the audience – trying to keep his distance from Lois. HE speaks urgently to the audience. LOIS pays no attention to him.*)

    DYSON. Mister Tomlinson has now run away. He will not get far. I intend to pursue him and carry out my orders expediently. In the meantime, however, I intend to eat my sack lunch. In much the same way a high performance vehicle must pull off the road, enabling the driver to rest and refuel, you are now encouraged to do the same. Thank you. (*Sits, removes a small paper sack from his coat. Inside the sack is a neatly wrapped sandwich and a small can of juice. HE tucks a paper napkin in his shirt, and eats as ...*)

(*HOUSE LIGHTS come up.*)

END OF ACT I

Note: *DYSON remains onstage, eating throughout the intermission.*
LOIS tends to the flower patch, then leaves to get something to drink.

ACT II

AT RISE: HOUSE LIGHTS fade. MISTER
DYSON has finished eating and is wiping his
mouth and hands thoroughly with his napkin.
LOIS is finishing her work on the flower bed.
DYSON stands and lifts his gun, speaking
urgently to the audience.)

DYSON. Hello again. Our brief rest is now
ended. I hope it was, for you, a productive and
invigorating detour. Now, please remain here as
I go in pursuit of Mister Tomlinson.

(DYSON starts off, LOIS speaks to the audience.
DYSON enters The Shadows.)

LOIS. Imagine. That man and I are going to
spend eternity up here. *(Pause.)* Sometimes, in the
afternoon, I make tuna. And we sit up here on an
old blanket and just look at things till it storms. I
love the storms. I'm not afraid of what's coming.
Jake's terrified. He's afraid that there is no
bowling in the world beyond. And what's worse,
he says, is that if they *do* bowl – they don't *keep*
score. If I had my way, we'd cover the Dust Bowl
with glass and open a greenhouse. Take up that

godawful turquoise carpet and take down that old
ball rack before it falls and kills somebody.

LORETTA. (*Enters wearing a Dust Bowl
warm-up jacket.*) Happy Birthday, kid.

LOIS. Happy Birthday yourself.

LORETTA. How you doin'?

LOIS. I'm kickin'.

LORETTA. Just passed that wild man you
call your husband. Told me I'd better be prepared
to bowl without the aid of God tonight.

LOIS. He's afraid that when you lose the
pastor, you lose the faith.

LORETTA. He's an odd one. Still don't know
why you married him.

LOIS. Somehow when you turn thirty, you
think that every train's the last one that's coming
by.

LORETTA. You shoulda held out for
Amtrack, instead of hoppin' a narrow gauge.

LOIS. C'mon, Loretta. You like Jake. I know
you do.

LORETTA. I like lightning, too. As long as
it's over there.

LOIS. You introduced me to him.

LORETTA. I apologize. My fault. I didn't
think you'd marry him.

LOIS. (*Sarcastic.*) Well, maybe you'll get
lucky and do better than I did.

LORETTA. I'm holdin' out for a big city man.
Spend a few years where you've got to lock your
doors and pick up after your dogs.

LOIS. Won't meet those guys on the bowling team.

LORETTA. Who knows? I heard Mudler's got another new crop of college guys from Duck Hollow.

LOIS. Have they been troweling the Vo-Tech again?

LORETTA. Yep.

LOIS. Keep you distance, Lois. You can hear those guys ticking.

LORETTA. Some of 'em are awful cute.

LOIS. Nice house, nobody home. I went out with a guy from the Duck Hollow Vo-Tech.

LORETTA. (*Not believing.*) When?

LOIS. About ten years ago. We went to a dance at the V.F.W. hall on the Fourth of July. All the guys came dressed as their favorite president. Half came as Washington. Half as Lincoln. Vo-Tech's not long in the history department. My date came as F.D.R. so he wouldn't have to dance. (*Pause.*) We sat for two hours in the corner, eating mints. Then he asked if I'd ever seen a "real ... smooth ... pickup." And I said maybe not, and he lifted me up over his head and took me out to the parking lot. That was pretty smooth, I said, and he said "That wasn't it. This is it." He pointed to his shiny silver Ford pickup truck with metallic green shell on back. "Want to get inside and get to know each other?" he said. Before I knew it, someone had sucked out all my common sense with a straw and I said "Sure" and we sat there

smelling the fresh vinyl seat covers. He didn't
say a word. I turned on the radio. He turned it off.
He said he had something to show me and he
unzipped his pants and reached way down in them
and pulled out a very ... small ...key. "This key
opens my gun rack" and sure enough there was
his twelve gauge shotgun locked to a rack behind
our heads and he took down that gun and began to
clean it with his white handkerchief. He
explained every detail of that gun to me during the
next hour as he caressed it with that
handkerchief. Then he loaded it. Then he lifted
the edge of my skirt with it and said "Now, what
are *you* gonna show *me*. (*Pause.*)

LORETTA. (*Impatient.*) Okay, okay. So,
what did you do?

LOIS. (*Pause.*) After showing him the entire
contents of my purse .. only four minutes had
elapsed. So, I started to unbutton my blouse. And
he started to smile. Then I stopped. I said "For the
good stuff we need to get in the back." "Under the
shell?" he said. "Yeah," I said. "I just put new
carpeting back there" he said. "Your choice," I
said, and after considering it for a moment ... he
nodded. "Take off all your clothes," I said. "Even
my shorts?" he said. "Especially your shorts," I
said. So there he was, naked in the back of the
shell. And there I was, about to climb in — when I
grabbed his clothes, slammed the cover shut,
locked him in and drove the pickup to the front
door of the V.F.W Hall. (*Stands.*) I walked

inside, grabbed the microphone from the stage and yelled "HEY, I GOT A KEG OF BEER IN THE BACK OF MY PICKUP. EVERYBODY HELP THEMSELVES." That metallic shell didn't last long, and F.D.R. would've been proud of how fast that boy ran away naked into the night.

LORETTA. (*Laughing, then stops.*) No.

LORETTA. Yeah.

(*THEY laugh.*)

LORETTA. Suppose he ever got over that?

LOIS. I don't think so. He still can't look me in the eye during his sermons.

LORETTA. (*Pause.*) that was Pastor Sod —

LOIS. Good ol' Sid.

LORETTA. NO.

LOIS. YEAH. He was born again shortly thereafter.

LORETTA. I've bowled with that man for years and I never knew.

LOIS. Now you do.

LORETTA. And he's still driving that pickup, isn't he?

LOIS. Yeah.

LORETTA. I will never again be able to keep a straight face during church.

LOIS. I know the feeling. You'll find it helps keep you awake, though.

LORETTA. (*Moving away.*) He's given me *rides home* in that pickup!

LOIS. Forget about it, Loretta. It's okay. What time is the big match tonight?

LORETTA. Seven-thirty. (*Takes off her Dust Bowl warm-up jacket to reveal her Dust Bowl bowling shirt — turquoise with bright orange letters.*) What do you think of our new shirts?

LOIS. Words cannot describe.

LORETTA. And the hand-embroidered name?

LOIS. (*Pause.*) What is my name doing on your shirt?

LORETTA. It's not my shirt. It's yours. Happy Birthday. (*Takes off the shirt, revealing an identical shirt of her own underneath.*)

LOIS. What are you doing, Loretta?

LORETTA. Molly and I decided you should be Sidney's substitute tonight. Put this on. (*Chasing Lois with the shirt.*)

LOIS. Wait.

LORETTA. C'mon, put this on.

LOIS. No.

LORETTA. Lois —

LOIS. Does Jake know about this?

LORETTA. He'll find out.

LOIS. (*Stops, turns to Loretta.*) That's what I'm afraid of. You've seen me bowl.

LORETTA. It was beautiful.

LOIS. Loretta, I am the only person in the history of the Dust Bowl to throw a ball that stopped before it got to the pins.

LORETTA. Lois, you'll be great. The human body is a bowling machine. *It knows how to bowl.* You just have to get out of its way. Now, put this on.

LOIS. Loretta, it's my birthday and I get to do whatever I want. And what I want is to stay home alone and do anything in the world other than make a fool of myself at the Dust Bowl.

LORETTA. It's my birthday, too. Don't I get what I want?

LOIS. I'm older. Deal with it.

LORETTA. It's just one night, Lois.

LOIS. Tell that to Jake. All he's talked about for a year is winning back that trophy.

LORETTA. You are more important to him than that trophy.

LOIS. Is that why my birthday got bumped to Thursday?

LORETTA. Let me just see if this fits.

LOIS. No way.

LORETTA. C'mon, Lois —

LOIS. No.

LORETTA. Please —

LOIS. NO.

LORETTA. (*Pause. Coyly, moving away.*) I'll tell Jake you went out with Pastor Sodderburger.

LOIS. That was ten years ago.

LORETTA. I might forget to tell him that part.

LOIS. Nothing happened.

LORETTA. That part, too.

LOIS. You would blackmail your best friend to get me to wear a stupid bowling shirt?

LORETTA. C'mon, it's not gonna kill you.

LOIS. Don't bet on it. (*Relents, puts the shirt on.*)

LORETTA. You look great.

LOIS. Thanks so much.

LORETTA. How do you feel?

LOIS. Give me a blindfold and a cigarette and lean me against a wall.

(*MOLLY enters on her bike with a wrapped package. SHE wears an identical bowling shirt with her name on it.*)

MOLLY. Hey, Mom. You look great.

LORETTA. (*To Lois.*) I told you.

MOLLY. Just wait till Dad sees you.

LOIS. That's what I keep thinking.

(*LORETTA gets the gift from Molly and brings it to Lois.*)

LORETTA. This is from Molly and me.

MOLLY. Dad paid for it, but he doesn't know it.

LOIS. I'm not in the mood for gifts.

MOLLY. You gotta open it. It's your birthday.

LOIS. Give it to Loretta.

LORETTA. Stop being such a brat and play along.

MOLLY. Yeah. Maybe you'll love it.

(Pause. LOIS unwraps the gift. It is a bowling ball bag with her name on it.)

LOIS. You are no longer my friends. Either of you.
MOLLY. Keep going.
LORETTA. It gets better.

(LOIS pulls a turquoise-speckled Voit bowling ball out of the bag. Long silence.)

MOLLY. No one in the league has a ball like that one.
LOIS. I can see why.
MOLLY. Go on, Mom. Try the fit.
LOIS. Which fingers?

(THEY stare at her.)

LOIS. Laugh. It's a joke.

(MOLLY and LORETTA smile and begin to sing, as LOIS holds the ball in front of her.)

LORETTA and MOLLY. "Happy Birthday to you. Happy Birthday to you. Happy Birthday dear Lois/Mom. Happy Birth —

(*JAKE appears. Singing stops abruptly. HE stares at Lois. SHE returns his stare. Silence.*)

LOIS. Hi, Jake.

JAKE. Lois.

LOIS. (*Pause.*) Find Pastor Sodderburger?

JAKE. No. His truck's already gone.

LOIS. What're you gonna do?

JAKE. (*Pause.*) Burn down the alley.

MOLLY. What?

JAKE. I'm not gonna be humiliated by a team from Mudler.

LORETTA. Lois is gonna bowl, Jake.

JAKE. (*Pause.*) Anybody got a match?

MOLLY. DAD.

JAKE. No way.

LORETTA. Why?

JAKE. Because we'll lose.

MOLLY. Loretta and I voted.

JAKE. SO?

LORETTA. So, this is our team. Let's go.

(*LORETTA and MOLLY begin to lead LOIS off. JAKE follows them.*)

JAKE. NO WAY.

MOLLY. She'll be great, Dad.

JAKE. She is not bowling on my team.

LORETTA. Then I am not bowling on your team.

MOLLY. Me neither.

LORETTA. Have a good time.

JAKE. WAIT A MINUTE.

LORETTA and MOLLY. BYE!

JAKE. NONE OF YOU UNDERSTAND WHAT THIS MEANS!

LOIS. (*Turning sharply on him.*) SHUT IT, JAKE! (*Pause.*) You want to know something? And don't answer that 'cause I don't care if you want to know it or not, 'cause I'm gonna tell you anyway and this is it —

JAKE. We don't have much time, Lois.

LOIS. Don't push me or you'll have eternity. (*Backing him Downstage with the bowling ball.*) Before I married you, Jake Tomlinson, I was a championship Whist player, a state doubles champ in horseshoes and I sang in the finest church choir in this county. Then, I let you be my Whist partner, my horseshoe partner, and the lead baritone in the choir. (*Pause.*) Jake, you are the worst card partner I've ever had and I've played with amnesiacs. You made me the laughingstock of the horseshoe circuit and luckily I won't have to put up with that anymore since you shattered those three windows last week. (*Pause.*) And did it ever occur to you why you're always a couple hours late to choir practice? *We tell you the wrong time, Jake.* Your singing turns glass black. (*Pause.*) So ... I am going to bowl on your team.

(*MOLLY and LORETTA cheer.*)

LOIS. And I am going to bowl the very best I can ... because that will guarantee my revenge. You just better hope I'm a faster learner than you are. Now, show me how to throw this thing. (*Tosses the ball to him.*)

(*Silence.*)

JAKE. (*Stares at Lois, then turns to Loretta and Molly.*) What time is it?
LORETTA. Seven twenty-five.
JAKE. Stall them.
MOLLY. How?
JAKE. Buy them drinks.
LORETTA. Okay.
JAKE. (*After a quick glance at Lois.*) *Many* drinks.
LORETTA. Relax, Jake, She'll be great.
MOLLY. See you there.

(*MOLLY and LORETTA leave. The bike remains behind. Long silence. JAKE walks up to Lois, holds the ball out to her. THEY both hold it for a moment, looking at each other.*)

JAKE. Okay. (*Pause.*) What is this?
LOIS. This is a bowling ball. You don't have to go *that* far back.
JAKE. No.
LOIS. No, *what?* It's *not* a bowling ball.

JAKE. No. (*Pause.*) This is death.

LOIS. Don't get weird on me, Jake. We've only got a couple minutes.

JAKE. This ball is death, Lois.

LOIS. Death would not wear turquoise.

JAKE. Put your fingers in.

(*SHE does. HE stands behind her as they face an imaginary lane that leads to the audience.*)

JAKE. Now. Do you see the kingpin?

LOIS. The what?

JAKE. The king. The five pin. Do you see it?

LOIS. No.

JAKE. Pretend.

LOIS. Okay. (*Stares front.*) I don't know which one is the five.

JAKE. The five is in the very center. Surrounded by a triangle of nine other pins. The five pin is protected.

LOIS. Okay.

JAKE. See it?

LOIS. Yeah.

JAKE. Good. (*Pause.*) You are the five pin.

LOIS. I am.

JAKE. Yeah.

LOIS. I thought I was holding death.

JAKE. You are.

LOIS. I can't do both things at once, Jake. It's confusing.

JAKE. Okay. Fine. I'll be the five pin, okay?

LOIS. Okay.

JAKE. (*Moving away and facing her.*) Fine. I am the five pin. I've got this shell, this protective family — like bodyguards — all around me. They'll fall before I will, even though the ball—

LOIS. Death.

JAKE. Right. Even though the ball is really lookin' to kill me. If I stay standing after death rolls through, I've won. The five pin is the key. Now, you've got two ways to kill me off: the left pocket or the right pocket.

LOIS. Where?

JAKE. Between the one and three pin which'd be called a perfect strike, or between the one and two pin which'd be called comin' in on the Brooklyn side. That's where I'm soft. Those three pins protect me — but if you find a seam between 'em, you got me. And if you got me, you more often than not have got the whole shootin' match. That clear?

LOIS. (*After a moment.*) I'm trying to kill you.

JAKE. Exactly.

LOIS. Somehow I'd feel less pressure if I just thought I was rolling a ball into some pins and trying to knock them down.

JAKE. (*Explodes.*) THAT'S HOW *AMATEURS* BOWL. AMATEURS THINK THIS IS A *GAME*. They do not understand the *stakes*. You gotta be ruthless and you gotta be clever. Otherwise, you're gonna thin-hit that one pin and leave yourself with a Heinz 57 or a Woolworth's five and dime. Or you're gonna nose-hit that one pin and be left with telephone poles. You want to sneak up on those pins and then POWERHOUSE 'em into that pit. You gotta roll a ball that has a mission, Lois. There is nothing more ruthless and clever than death ... so, think of your ball as death. When you swing your arm back like this you are holding power in your hand, and when you release that ball you are releasing a power that will change the way everything has been so carefully arranged. SHATTER IT. TIME AND TIME AGAIN. DEATH, LOIS. (*Pause.*) That clear?

(*Pause, LOIS stares at the bowling ball.*)

JAKE. You nervous? (*Pause.*) Don't be nervous. You'll be great.
LOIS. What if they laugh at me?
JAKE. Laugh right back.
LOIS. What if you laugh at me.
JAKE. (*Pause.*) I never will.
LOIS. (*Pause.*) That's nice.
JAKE. (*Pause.*) 'Cause you're not very funny.
LOIS. (*Tosses the ball to him.*) Good catch.
JAKE. So are you.

(*THEY kiss, embrace. MOLLY appears.*)

MOLLY. Good technique, wrong sport. C'mon, they're waiting.

(*MOLLY runs off. JAKE stares at Lois.*)

JAKE. (*To Lois.*) You ready?

(*JAKE and LOIS go down the hill, arm in arm. DYSON steps out of The Shadows and watches them go down the hill, sees the bike, mounts it and starts off after them. Stops. Turns to audience.*)

DYSON. As I seek to carry out my mission, let me make an observation. Strange things seem to happen here. I am reminded of the haunting sensation of driving a deserted road through dense fog, where – being unable to see even the front of one's own car – one simply trusts that the earth is flat and that roads are straight and one simply hopes that the automobile is capable of swerving quickly enough to avoid oncoming headlights. (*Pause.*) Fog is the only natural element that makes all cars equal. In the fog, everyone drives a Corvair.

(*DYSON starts down the hill on the bike. Sees someone coming. Stops. Dismounts bike and hides in The Shadows, as JAKE appears. JAKE walks slowly and deliberately to the lawn chair at center. Looks at it. Sits. Stares front. DYSON starts to move in. MOLLY appears. DYSON retreats.*)

MOLLY. (*Looks at Jake for a moment, then speaks softly to him.*) Dad? (*Pause.*) Daddy? (*Pause.*) You okay? (*Pause, turns to audience.*) He got what he wanted ... and he lost it. Lois outbowled everyone. The Mudler team left town in shame. The trophy was ours once again. And Dad was in all his glory. So, when Lois suggested we drive up to Gleason to celebrate, Dad said "Bring that trophy along with you. Let's show it off a little bit." (*Pause.*) The storm had started a few minutes earlier. We all ran out in the rain, across the parking lot to the Rambler – with Lois holding the trophy high above her head. (*Pause.*) For a second. (*Pause.*) That was the brightest light I have ever seen. (*Pause.*) We buried her up here. And a few weeks later, Loretta became a victim of only the second bowling ball rack collapse in modern history. That was a year ago and Dad has hardly said a word about it. Till today.

JAKE. I hate that goddamn alley, Molly.

MOLLY. I know you do.

JAKE. It's lost me everything I ever loved except you – and in two years when you graduate, it'll be a clean sweep.

MOLLY. I'm got goin' anywhere, Dad.

JAKE. Sure you are. You gotta see what's out there. And when you do, keep one thing in mind: don't dive for any foul balls – it's just not worth it.

MOLLY. Dad, let's go down and make some supper or something, okay?

JAKE. (*Looking around.*) WHOEVER KNOWS THINGS has got secrets they're not telling. SOMEONE'S LYING IN WAIT FOR ME. "Sky and Earth and finally Water" – hell, it don't take someone from Wyoming to figure out that that prophecy was not Maggie's. It's mine. IT'S A DEATH PROPHECY. AND THIS, MOLLY, THIS IS THE TENTH FRAME.

(*JAKE suddenly begins raking and shovelling Lois' grave. HE will do this – burying the geraniums in the process – until it once again resembles a mound of earth with only the pinwheel as its headstone.*
From offstage, we hear LOIS and LORETTA singing "Bye Bye Blackbird" softly, in the distance.
MOLLY tries to get Jake's attention.)

MOLLY. Dad, it's Teen Night. You comin' down? Daddy? I gotta go stock the frozen pizzas. (*Goes down the hill on her bike.*)

(*Offstage SINGING continues.*)

JAKE. (*Still working on Lois' grave.*) The sky killed Lois. Don't think it didn't. Taking with it the best alto in the choir and one of the most promising new bowlers in this region. (*Moves to*

Loretta's grave and rebuilds it, as he did Lois'.)
Loretta was killed by the earth. The tree I made
that ball rack from grew right out of the earth on
my property. The earth got her, all right. Taking
with it a gifted hairdresser and the only existing
recipe to the finest loaf of bread in this region.
*(Continues his work till finished. HE then holds
the shovel as a weapon and sits in the chair.)*

(Offstage SINGING continues.)

   JAKE. I will not be the third. WHOEVER
KNOWS THINGS wants me to break down like
my daddy and try to walk across Moby Lake
where the WATER is waiting there to kill me. But
I will conquer that authentic gypsy woman and
her two-bit prophecy if I have to avoid every drop of
water for the rest of my life. I'll lay by enough
Fresca to go the distance.

(Offstage SINGING stops abruptly.
DYSON begins to approach Jake from behind,
*   holding the gun close to his body, but keeping*
*   it pointed at Jake. His approach takes the*
*   entire speech.)*

   JAKE. *(To audience, very confident.)*
WHOEVER KNOWS THINGS is not gonna
break me. Not gonna take away my Dust Bowl.
Not gonna stop me from falling in love just
because every time I do there is a natural disaster

resulting in death. (*Pause.*) Who the hell ever said you had to love just one person this life? Good lord, imagine the pressure on that person. It ain't natural to spend years tryin' to fall in love with someone, then meet 'em and fall in love with 'em, and then spend years trying NOT to fall in love with someone *else*. (*Proudly.*) Me, I've fallen stupid-face-first-on-the-pavement in love three times so far this life. And I expect to wake up in the morning, walk down to the mailbox or somewhere, look up ... and catch a glance from some woman with out-of-state plates. And if there's enough *glance* in that glance and enough gas in my Rambler — I just might have a new name on my lips come nightfall. (*Pause.*) I spent years tryin' to get Maggie's first glance back. That glance was the best moment of our whole damn lives. There was never more mystery, there was never more nothin'. After the glance, the rest is just connect-the-dots. (*Sets the shovel to one side and opens his* Reader's Digest.)

[Note: Ideally, the stage should look identical at this point to the way it did in the beginning — just before Molly's lullaby put Jake to sleep.]

JAKE. Course, I'll have to warn the next person I meet about the dangers of marryin' a guy like me. They got a right to know. And if next time I get nothin' more than just the glance ... I'll just have to make that be enough. (*Looks at the* Digest *and begins to close his eyes.*)

(*DYSON is only a few feet from Jake. MOLLY appears on her bike and sees Dyson.*)

MOLLY. DAD, LOOK OUT!
JAKE. Relax, Molly. I'm fine.
MOLLY. DAD!
JAKE. Don't worry, anymore. I've beat that paranoia thing.
MOLLY. BUT DAD –
JAKE. I've got everything under control now.
MOLLY. – HE'S GOT A GUN!

(*JAKE turns and sees DYSON holding the gun a few feet from him. JAKE jumps up and holds the lawn chair in front of his body for protection. MOLLY stands frozen by her bicycle.*)

DYSON. Are you Mister Jake Tomlinson?
JAKE. Yeah – uh, NO.
DYSON. I'm Mister Dyson. Please call me that. I was sent for you. I have been waiting here.
JAKE. Where?
DYSON. In The Shadows.
JAKE. Look, Mister –
DYSON. Dyson.

JAKE. – you haven't got a chance. I am a – (*Pause.*) I am a well known – (*Pause, looks at Molly.*) My *daughter* is a well known black belt.

DYSON. (*Glancing at Molly.*) Are you serious?

JAKE. Absolutely.

DYSON. Great. I'll have someone to practice with.

JAKE. Look, uh, buddy – I don't want to have to call in my goons.

DYSON. Feel free to call. I have all day. And I have a phone in my briefcase. (*Pulls antenna out of the top of his briefcase.*)

JAKE. Look, uh, old friend – you don't really want to shoot that gun, do you?

DYSON. What?

JAKE. The gun. Why don't you put it away?

DYSON. I can't.

JAKE. Sure you can.

DYSON. No, I can't.

JAKE. WHY?

DYSON. It's for you.

(*DYSON hands Jake the gun. JAKE takes it, disbelieving.*)

DYSON. Thanks. Those things give me the creeps. It is reminiscent of the feeling one has when your left-turn signal sticks and you are forced to disengage it manually. Corner after corner. That sort of creeps.

JAKE. Uh ... yeah. Molly, come here.

(*MOLLY runs to his side. JAKE lowers the lawn chair.*)

DYSON. Now. Are you Mister Jake Tomlinson?
JAKE. Uh ... yeah.
DYSON. And are you Molly Tomlinson?
MOLLY. How do you know us?
DYSON. Just a moment.

(*DYSON reaches into his pocket. Instantly, JAKE crouches behind the lawn chair, pointing the gun at Dyson. MOLLY hides behind Jake.*
DYSON pulls a small key out of his pocket and show it to them. THEY relax a bit. DYSON unlock the handcuffs with the key. Legs unfold from the briefcase, so that it stands on its own. The same key opens the briefcase and when open, a small LAMP rises from the case and shines down into it. The effect is that of a miniature office.)

DYSON. Have a seat, Mister Tomlinson, will you?

(*JAKE sits in the chair. MOLLY stands behind him.*)

DYSON. I was, until a few days ago, an employee of Ms. Maggie O'Connell. The former Ms. Maggie Tomlinson. I was dispatched to find you and bring you several items. The first item being the gun.

JAKE. For god sakes why?

(*DYSON lifts an envelope from the briefcase and shows it to Jake and Molly.*)

DYSON. So, in case I try to run away with this, you can fire a brief warning shot and then fell me in my tracks. In much the same way an automobile may be struck down by a sudden tire dysfunction on the expressway. Is that clear?

JAKE. Uh ... yeah.

(*DYSON holds the envelope aloft, then jerks his body to one side as if to run away. JAKE immediately pulls the gun out and aims it at Dyson. DYSON turns to Jake and smiles.*)

DYSON. Good. Very good. Here you are.

(*DYSON hands the envelope to Jake. JAKE looks at it, looks at Dyson, then hands it to MOLLY who opens it quickly.*)

MOLLY. Oh my god.
JAKE. (*Still looking at Dyson.*) What?
MOLLY. Oh my god, Dad.

JAKE. What?
MOLLY. I don't believe it.
JAKE. WHAT!

(*MOLLY hands Jake the paper, THEY both stare at it.*)

JAKE. (*Overwhelmed.*) Three hundred and fifty thousand dollars.

(*Brief pause. Then JAKE and MOLLY erupt into SCREAMS, CHEERS, and hugs.*)

JAKE. I LOVE THAT WOMAN. GODDAMNIT, I LOVE THAT WOMAN!
MOLLY. Three hundred and fifty thousand dollars! WHOOO-HOOOOOOOO!
JAKE. (*Overlapping.*) I TAKE BACK EVERYTHING I EVER SAID. I ALWAYS LOVED THAT WOMAN!
MOLLY. (*Overlapping.*) WE'RE RICH. WE CAN GET RID OF THE RAMBLER!
JAKE. (*Overlapping.*) WHOOOO-EEEEEEE!

(*As MOLLY is giving Dyson a quick kiss on the cheek, JAKE freezes. Then sits abruptly in the chair.*)

DYSON. I'm glad your pleased.
JAKE. We can't take it.
MOLLY. DAD?!

DYSON. What's that, sir?

JAKE. I took charity from that woman once and everything has been miserable since.

MOLLY. DAD!!!

JAKE. We can't take it, Molly. This is not our money and this is not something we need.

MOLLY. (*Grabbing for the check.*) Then I'll take it!

JAKE. (*Pulling it away from her reach.*) No. We are above this and I don't know who your mother thinks she is or what gave her the idea that she could buy us off with over a quarter million measly dollars! Thank you, Mr. Dyson, but our answer to you is NO. (*Begins tearing the check into tiny pieces.*) NO. NO. NO. NO. NO. NO. NO. NO. NO. (*Scatters the bits of paper all over the ground.*)

MOLLY. DAD, WHAT ARE YOU THINKING? WHY DID YOU DO THAT?

(*Long silence.*)

JAKE. I really don't know, Molly. That was the stupidest thing I have ever done.

(*Long silence. DYSON pulls an identical envelope out of the briefcase.*)

DYSON. Well. Anticipating your response, your former wife enclosed this.

(*DYSON hands the envelope to Jake, who opens it quickly.*)

JAKE. New check. Same amount. (*Kisses the check.*) GOD, I LOVE THAT WOMAN!

MOLLY. Why would she send us that now?
JAKE. Doesn't matter, kiddo. Now we are big time. Now we put in computerized scoreboards.
MOLLY. (*To Dyson.*) Who are you?
DYSON. Mister Dyson. Please call me that.
MOLLY. What do you do?
DYSON. I drive.
JAKE. So? Who doesn't?
DYSON. I drive *well*. I graduated with honors from the Samuel Crocker School of Automotive Operation. Class president. Editor of the Road Review. Until three days ago, I was Ms. Maggie O'Connell's private chauffeur.
JAKE. Now what are you?

(*DYSON takes off his sunglasses for the first time.*)

DYSON. Based on a stipulation in Ms. O'Connell's will, I now work for you.

(*Silence.*)

JAKE. What will?
MOLLY. (*Soft.*) I don't want to hear this.

(*Silence.*)

JAKE. Answer me, Dyson.
DYSON. Ms. O'Connell's private schooner encountered bad weather off the Greek island of Mykonos and subsequently sank. There were no known survivors. Her body has yet to be found.

(*JAKE and MOLLY hold each other.*)

DYSON. Tucked away in her safe deposit box — in much the same way one tucks away their car registration safely in the glove compartment — were three items. (*Reaches into the briefcase.*) The first item is a key.

(*DYSON hands the key — tied to an old shoestring — to Jake. JAKE hands it to Molly. It looks identical to the one she wears around her neck. SHE carries it to the bicycle and opens the lock with it. SHE puts the shoestring around her neck and stares at the bike.*)

MOLLY. Dad, get rid of this bike. I don't want it anymore.
JAKE. Molly —
MOLLY. Please, Dad.
JAKE. You've had that bike for —
MOLLY. I don't want it. I don't want to look at it anymore.

(*JAKE looks at her, then wheels the bike Upstage between Lois and Loretta's graves.*)

DYSON. The second item is a sealed letter.

(*DYSON hands the letter to MOLLY who opens it. LIGHTS focus on her downstage as, in DIM LIGHT, JAKE buries the bike in the center grave.*)

MOLLY. "Dear Molly, I guess it's true that everyone has one letter in them that they never mail. And then one day when it's too late to make a difference, that letter falls into the right hands. I hope it's not too late.

"I never liked your father. I loved him like mad, but I never learned to like him. I resented the fact that I never had so much fun in my life as when I lived with him. I always thought there was supposed to be more to it than that.

"Fun is enough, Molly. Everything else is theory.

"I could turn any situation into a catastrophe and your father could turn that same situation into fun. Like when we discovered that the only thing that would settle your stomach on long car trips was peppermint schnapps. We'd pull over in some postage stamp town, and I'd put on dark glasses and sneak into the liquor store, come out with a brown paper sack and a plastic spoon, crouch down with you in the back seat and try to keep my hand from shaking as I raised the spoon to your mouth. That was a catastrophe till your father got a hold of it. Next time you felt sick, he'd stop the car in front of the local tavern, march us in and plop us down on three barstools. 'Schnapps. Three shots,' he'd say. We'd lift our glasses and he'd say, 'Mud in your eye. Bowl free or die.' And we'd down our schnapps in front of some disbelieving bartender. 'Pay the man, Maggie,' he'd say. 'Let's go kid. You'll be fine.' And off you two went, laughing all the way to the car.

"Your father has a way with a situation.

"Don't spend your whole life in Turtle Rapids. And don't spend your whole life away, afraid to go home, either. And don't put roses on my grave.

"You've always been in my thoughts, and if after all these years I'm still in yours – *have fun*. And when fun stops, get on a train.

"Love, Mom.

"P.S. – Try to get your dad interested in a new sport. Something less competitive. He'll live longer."

(*JAKE has finished burying the bike. HE puts the third pinwheel at the head of the center grave.*
A BREEZE comes up and spins the pinwheels.
The LIGHTS have gradually shifted to moonlight.
JAKE walks up to Molly and holds her.)

DYSON. The third and final item is this.
(*Reaches into his briefcase and pulls out a Glow-In-The-Dark Frisbee.*)

JAKE. We already got Tupperware.
MOLLY. Dad, it's a Frisbee.
JAKE. What's it *do*?
MOLLY. (*Takes the Frisbee from Dyson.*)
Stand over there.
JAKE. Why?
MOLLY. Just do. Stand over there by Lois
JAKE. Lois is on this side?
MOLLY. Yeah. And Loretta's —
JAKE. Over there, I knew that.
MOLLY. I'm gonna stand here and we're
gonna throw this thing.
JAKE. If we disrupt their graves, they'll kill
me.
MOLLY. You gotta beat this paranoia thing,
Dad. Here we go.

(*THEY are on either side of the stage with the
graves between them.*
*DYSON sits Downstage in the lawn chair. HE
watches them.*
*MOLLY throws the Frisbee to Jake who catches it
awkwardly. HE throws it back.*)

JAKE. (*After a few throws.*) So, tell me
something, Molly.
MOLLY. What?

JAKE. How do you score this thing?
MOLLY. You don't.
JAKE. Then why do you do it?
MOLLY. You just do

(*THEY continue to play.*)

DYSON. Mister Tomlinson?
JAKE. Yes, Mister Dyson?
DYSON. Regarding the provision wherein you become responsible for my employment –
JAKE. You ever set pins, Mister Dyson?
DYSON. What's that, sir?
JAKE. Pins. You ever set 'em?
DYSON. No, sir.
JAKE. You'll learn.
DYSON. I've set points and plugs.
JAKE. Close enough.
DYSON. And in many ways the black limousine is the automotive equivalent of the standard black bowling ball. Simple, yet strong. Deceptive, yet destructive. And the act of bowling itself is not unlike hurtling down the expressway to collide with some far distant destination. There is, in each, a certain inevitability. One accepts that, and then relishes the moment of impact.
JAKE. Mister Dyson.
DYSON. Yes, sir.
JAKE. Take the night off.
DYSON. Thank you, sir. (*Turns off the LAMP in his briefcase, then closes the case. HE*

turns to the audience.) He has now given me the night off. You are on your own. Goodnight. And drive safely.

(*DYSON takes out his harmonica and begins to softly play "Bye Bye Blackbird."*
The pinwheels continue to SPIN.
JAKE and MOLLY continue the rhythmic throwing of the Frisbee.)

MOLLY. Dad?

JAKE. Yeah, Molly.

MOLLY. You sure you haven't played this before?

JAKE. I'm sure.

MOLLY. Just comes natural, huh?

JAKE. Thanks to the Louie Twinkler all-purpose sports hand.

MOLLY. (*Laughs.*) I still don't believe that story.

JAKE. You will if you ever tell it. (*Pause.*) You sure there ain't a way to score this?

MOLLY. Yeah.

JAKE. Than what's the object?

MOLLY. Don't let it hit the ground.

(*DYSON continues the song.*
LIGHTS fade until nothing can be seen but the
   moon and the moving Frisbee.)

END OF PLAY

COSTUME PLOT

JAKE:
(ACT I)
Overalls, T-shirt, Work boots, Feed cap, Clean white shirt
(ACT II)
Work pants, Bowling shirt (turquoise with "Dust Bowl" logo), Work boots

MOLLY:
(ACT I)
Jeans, Sweatshirt, Sneakers
(ACT II)
Bowling shirt (identical to Jake's)

LOIS:
(ACT I)
Shorts, Cotton shirt, Sandals
(ACT II)
Bowling shirt (identical to Jake's)

LORETTA:
(ACT I)
Tight jeans, Tank top, Loose shirt (over tank top), Cowboy boots
(ACT II)
Bowling shirt (identical to Jake's), Warm-up jacket (similar to shirt, with logo)

MISTER DYSON:
(ACT I)
Black three-piece suit, Blood-red tie, Black
fedora, Black leather gloves, Dark sunglasses,
Black dress shoes
(ACT II)
Same

PROPERTY PLOT

JAKE: Shovel, Rake, Lawn Chair, *Reader's Digest*, Can of Fresca

MOLLY: Bicycle, with basket on front, Bicycle padlock and chain, Bowling Pins with Pinwheels rising out of the top (3), Key on string around neck

MISTER DYSON: Briefcase, with light and built-in stand, Handcuffs, Revolver in shoulder holster, Bullets for revolver, Key to handcuffs, Letter to Molly (in envelope), $350,000 check (in envelope) -- torn nightly, (replacement check), Harmonica, Glow-in-the-dark Frisbee

LOIS: Geraniums in clay pots (3), Trowel

LORETTA: Geraniums in clay pots (3), Trowel, Bowling Bag (wrapped as gift), Bowling Ball (turquoise speckled)

Preset: Plastic straw (sticking up from center grave)

AUTHOR'S NOTE ON SET

The set, while being primarily realistic, should convey a sense of mystery, a sense of danger lurking somewhere about. The necessary elements are three unmarked graves which are covered with dirt, a path which leads down the hill and offstage, and an upstage area given over to trees and brush which is knows as The Shadows.

The center of the three graves must be rigged in such a way that Jake can make his initial entrance up through the grave, and that, in Act II, Molly's bicycle can be buried in the same spot. Most productions of the play have used either a raked stage, or a trap underneath this center grave to achieve the desired effect. The dirt on the grave is held in place by either cloth or rubber which can open, like a sphincter, at the stated moments. Several designers have found that the ground-up rubber from old tires was preferable to using actual dirt on the graves.

Other Publications for Your Interest

OTHER PEOPLE'S MONEY
(LITTLE THEATRE—DRAMA)

By JERRY STERNER

3 men, 2 women—One Set

Wall Street takeover artist Lawrence Garfinkle's intrepid computer is going "tilt" over the undervalued stock of New England Wire & Cable. He goes after the vulnerable company, buying up its stock to try and take over the company at the annual meeting. If the stockholders back Garfinkle, they will make a bundle—but what of the 1200 employees? What of the local community? Too bad, says Garfinkle, who would then liquidate the company—take the money and run. Set against the charmingly rapacious financier are Jorgenson, who has run the company since the Year One and his chief operations officer, Coles, who understands, unlike the genial Jorgenson, what a threat Garfinkle poses to the firm. They bring in Kate, a bright young woman lawyer, who specializes in fending off takeovers—and who is the daughter of Jorgenson's administrative assistant, Bea. Kate must not only contend with Garfinkle—she must also move Jorgenson into taking decisive action. Should they use "greenmail"? Try to find a "White Knight"? Employ a "shark repellent"? This compelling drama about Main Street vs. Wall Street is as topical and fresh as today's headlines, giving its audience an inside look at what's *really going on* in this country and asking trenchant questions, not the least of which is whether a corporate raider is really the creature from the Black Lagoon of capitalism or the Ultimate Realist come to save business from itself.

(#17064)

THE DOWNSIDE
(LITTLE THEATRE—COMEDY)

By RICHARD DRESSER

6 men, 2 women—Combination Interior

These days, American business is a prime target for satire, and no recent play has cut as deep, with more hilarious results, than this superb new comedy from the Long Wharf Theatre, Mark & Maxwell, a New Jersey pharmaceuticals firm, has acquired U.S. rights to market an anti-stress drug manufactured in Europe, pending F.D.A. approval; but the marketing executives have got to come up with a snazzy ad campaign by January—and here we are in December! The irony is that nowhere is this drug more needed than right there at Mark & Maxwell, a textbook example of corporate ineptitude, where it seems all you have to do to get ahead is look good in a suit. The marketing strategy meetings get more and more pointless and frenetic as the deadline approaches. These meetings are "chaired" by Dave, the boss, who is never actually there—he is a voice coming out of a box, as Dave phones in while jetting to one meeting or another, eventually directing the ad campaign on his mobile phone while his plane is being hijacked! Doesn't matter to Dave, though—what matters is the possible "downside" of this new drug: hallucinations. "Ridiculous", says the senior marketing executive Alan: who then proceeds to tell how Richard Nixon comes to his house in the middle of the night to visit..."Richard Dresser's deft satirical sword pinks the corporate image repeatedly, leaving the audience amused but thoughtful."—Meriden Record. "Funny and ruthlessly cynical."—Phila. Inquirer. "A new comedy that is sheer delight."—Westport News. "The Long Wharf audience laughed a lot, particularly those with office training. But they were also given something to ponder about the way we get things done in America these days, or rather pretend to get things done. No wonder the Japanese are winning."—L.A. Times.

(#6718)

Other Publications for Your Interest

LLOYD'S PRAYER
(LITTLE THEATRE—COMEDY)
By KEVIN KLING

3 men, 1 woman (1 man & 1 woman play various parts). Bare stage w/set pieces.

Be amazed! The author of the amazing *21A* has fashioned a hilarious comic parable about Bob, the Raccoon Boy, and what happens to him when he is "rescued" from the raccoons who raised him and taught what it means to be human. At first, Bob can only make whirring raccoon sounds, but he is taught to speak by a delightfully whacko "Mom and Dad". He is taken from his cage at Mom and Dad's house by an ambitious ex-con named Lloyd, who sees the raccoon boy as his ticket to fame and fortune. When his first idea—displaying Bob as a carny sideshow freak—fails, Lloyd gets the brilliant idea to become a religious evangelist, displaying Bob as another sort of freak: a miracle from God. Lloyd's pitch, a promise of inspiration "that will bring grown men to a sitting position and women to a greater understanding of themselves", makes them both celebrities. By this time, Bob speaks pretty well ("I've been called many things in my life . . . But I prefer 'Bob'"), and is on the verge of innocence corrupted when there appears on the scene a beautiful guardian angel, dressed as a high school cheerleader. "Be amazed!", she declares, admonishing Bob to beware of Lloyd. What ensues is an amusing tug-of-war between the angel and Lloyd, with Bob the Raccoon Boy as the rope. The unqualified hit of the Actors Theatre of Louisville 1988 Humana Festival, this brilliant new comedy is "a whirlwind of original humor that comes in waves."—Lexington Herald-Leader. "Fresh, funny and charming."—Columbus Dispatch. "Kling is quite simply a comic genius."—Dramatics Magazine.

(#13997)

21A
(ADVANCED GROUPS—COMEDY)
By KEVIN KLING

1 man—Bare stage w/chairs.

"Astonishing", was the way Newsweek Magazine summed up this one-man tour-de-force in which Mr. Kling performed all the riders on a Minneapolis city bus: eight characters, including the driver. Structured as a series of monologues which in "real life" are going on simultaneously, this hilarious and decidedly "different" play had them rolling in the aisles at Louisville's famed Humana Festival where it won the prestigious Heideman Award. Kling started with the droll driver and moved on to such odd-balls as Gladys, Chairman Francis (a religious proselytizer), Captain Twelve-Pack (a drunk with a beer 12-pack box over his head) and a businessman who is decidedly *not* "Dave", no matter how fervently Captain Twelve-Pack insists that he *is*. And: who is the mysterious intruder sitting at the back of the bus? "Stunning."—U.S.A. Today.

(#22237)